The Poetry of Bliss Carman

Volume IV - More Songs From Vagabondia

Co-Authored with Richard Hovey

William Bliss Carman was born in Fredericton, in New Brunswick on April 15th 1861. He was educated at Fredericton Collegiate School before moving to the University of New Brunswick, obtaining his B.A. there in 1881. As is common with so many writers his first published piece was for the University magazine and for Carman that was in 1879.

After several years editing various magazines and periodicals Carman first published a poetry volume in 1893 with Low Tide on Grand Pré. There was no Canadian company prepared to publish and when an American company did so it went bankrupt.

The following year was decidedly better. His partnership with the American poet Richard Hovey had given birth to Songs of Vagabondia. It was an immediate success.

That success prompted the Boston firm, Stone & Kimball, to reissue Low Tide on Grand Pré and to hire Carman as the editor of its literary journal, The Chapbook.

Carman brought out, in 1895, Behind the Arras, a somewhat more serious and philosophical work centered on the premise of a long meditation, using the speaker's house and its many rooms, as a symbol of life and the choices to be made.

In 1896 Carman met Mrs Mary Perry King, who rapidly became patron, adviser and sometime lover. She also became his writing collaborator on two verse dramas.

In 1897 Carman published Ballad of Lost Haven, and in 1898, By the Aurelian Wall, the title poem itself was an elegy to John Keats and the book was a collection of formal elegies.

As the century turned Carman was hard at work on a five-volume set of poetry "Pans Pipes". The excellence of a number of these poems did much to install Carman as the most noted of Canadian Poets and eventually their own Poet Laureate.

In 1912 the final work in the Vagabondia series was published. Richard Hovey had died in 1900 and so this last work was purely Carman's. It has a distinct elegiac tone as if remembering the past works themselves.

On October 28th, 1921 Carman was honored by the newly-formed Canadian Authors' Association where he was crowned Canada's Poet Laureate with a wreath of maple leaves.

William Bliss Carman died of a brain hemorrhage at the age of 68 in New Canaan on the 8th June, 1929.

And ever with the vanguard
The vagrant singers come

The gamins of the city
Who dance before the drum

Index of Contents

JONGLEURS

What is the stir in the street?
Hurry of feet!
And after,
A sound as of pipes and of tabers!

Men of the conflicts and labors,
Struggling and shifting and shoving,
Pushing and pounding your neighbors,
Fighting for leeway for laughter,
Toiling for leisure for loving!
Hark, through the window and up to the rafter,
Madder and merrier,
Deeper and verier,
Sweeter, contrarier,
Dafter and dafter,
A song arises,—
A thrill, an intrusion,
A reel, an illusion,
A rapture, a crisis
Of bells in the air!

Ay, up from your work and look out of the window!
"Who are the newcomers, Arab or Hindoo?
Persians, or Japs, or the children of Isis?"
—Guesses, surmises—
Forth with you, fare
Down in the street to draw nearer and stare!
Come from your palaces, come from your hovels!
Lay down your ledgers, your picks and your shovels,

Your trowels and bricks,
Hammers and nails,
Scythes and flails,
Bargains and sales,
And the trader's tricks,
Deals, overreachings,
Worries and griefs,
Teachings and preachings,
Boluses, briefs,
Writs and attachments,
Quarterings, hatchments,
Clans and cognomens,
Comments and scholia,
(World's melancholia)—
Cast them aside, and good riddance to rubbish!
Here at the street-corner, hearken, a strain,
Rough and off-hand and a bit rub-a-dub-ish,
Gives us a taste of the life we'd attain.

Who are they, what are they, whence have they come to us?
Where will they go when their singing is done?
What is the garb they wear, tattered and sumptuous,
Faded with days and superb in the sun?
What are they singing of?
Hush!
... There's a ringing of
Delicate chimes;
And the blush
Of a veiled bride morning
Beats in the rhymes.
Listen!
Out of the merriment,
Clear as the glisten
Of dew on the brier,
A silver warning!
Sudden, a dare—
Lyric experiment—
Up like a lark in the air,
Higher and higher and higher,
The song shoots out of our blunder
Of thought to the blue sky of wonder,
And broken strains only fall down
Like pearls on the roofs of the town.

Somebody says they have come from the moon,
Seen with their eyes Eldorado,
Sat in the Bo-tree's shadow,
Wandered at noon

In the valleys of Van,
Tented in Lebanon, tarried in Ophir,
Last year in Tartary piped for the Khan.
Now it's the song of a lover;
Now it's the lilt of a loafer,—
Under the trees in a midsummer noon,
Dreaming the haze into isles to discover,
Beating the silences into a croon;
Soon
Up from the marshes a fall of the plover!
Out from the cover
A flurry of quail!
Down from the height where the slow hawks hover,
The thin far ghost of a hail!
And near, and near,
Throbbing and tingling,—
With a human cheer
In the earth-song mingling,—
Mirth and carousal,
Wooing, espousal,
Clinking of glasses
And laughter of lasses—
And the wind in the garden stoops down as it passes
To play with the hair
Of the loveliest there,
And the wander-lust catches the will in its snare;
Hill-wind and spray-lure,
Call of the heath;
Dare in the teeth
Of the balk and the failure;
The clasp and the linger
Of loosening finger,
Loth to dissever;
Thrill of the comrade heart to its fellow
Through droughts that sicken and blasts that bellow
From purple furrow to harvest yellow,
Now and forever.
How our feet itch to keep time to their measure!
How our hearts lift to the lilt of their song!
Let the world go, for a day's royal pleasure!
Not every summer such waifs come along.

Now they are off to the inn;
Hear the clean ring of their laughter!
Cool as a hill-brook after
The beat of the noon sets in!
Gentlemen even in jollity—
Certainly people of quality!—

Waifs and estrays no less,
Roofless and penniless,
They are the wayside strummers
Whose lips are man's renown,
Those wayward brats of Summer's
Who stroll from town to town;
Spendthrift of life, they ravish
The days of an endless store,
And ever the more they lavish
The heap of the hoard is more.
For joy and love and vision
Are alive and breed and stay
When dust shall hold in derision
The misers of a day.

EARTH'S LYRIC

April. You hearken, my fellow,
Old slumberer down in my heart?
There's a whooping of ice in the rivers;
The sap feels a start.

The snow-melted torrents are brawling;
The hills, orange-misted and blue,
Are touched with the voice of the rainbird
Unsullied and new.

The houses of frost are deserted,
Their slumber is broken and done,
And empty and pale are the portals
Awaiting the sun.

The bands of Arcturus are slackened;
Orion goes forth from his place
On the slopes of the night, leading homeward
His hound from the chase.

The Pleiades weary and follow
The dance of the ghostly dawn;
The revel of silence is over;
Earth's lyric comes on.

A golden flute in the cedars,
A silver pipe in the swales,
And the slow large life of the forest
Wells bade and prevails.

A breath of the woodland spirit
Has blown out the bubble of spring
To this tenuous hyaline glory
One touch sets a-wing.

THE WOOD-GOD.

Brother, lost brother!
Thou of mine ancient kin!
Thou of the swift will that no ponderings smother!
The dumb life in me fumbles out to the shade
Thou lurkest in.
In vain—evasive ever through the glade
Departing footsteps fail;
And only where the grasses have been pressed,
Or by snapped twigs I follow a fruitless trail.
So—give o'er the quest!
Sprawl on the roots and moss!
Let the lithe garter squirm across my throat!
Let the slow clouds and leaves above me float
Into mine eyeballs and across,—
Nor think them further! Lo, the marvel! now,
Thou whom my soul desireth, even thou
Sprawl'st by my side, who fled'st at my pursuit.
I hear thy fluting; at my shoulder there
I see the sharp ears through the tangled hair,
And birds and bunnies at thy music mute.

A FAUN'S SONG

Cool! cool! cool!
Cool and sweet
The feel of the moss at my feet!
And sweet and cool
The touch of the wind, of the wind!

Cool wind out of the blue,
At the touch of you
A little wave crinkles and flows
All over me down to my toes.

"Coo-loo! Coo-loo!"
Hear the doves in the tree-tops croon.

"Coo-loo! Coo-loo!"
Love comes soon.

"June! June!"
The veery sings,
Sings and sings,
"June! June!"—
A pretty tune!

Wind with your weight of perfume,
Bring me the bluebells' bloom!

QUINCE TO LILAC: To G. H.

Dear Lilac, how enchanting
To hear of you this way!
The Man who comes a-mouching
To visit me each day

Says you too have a lover
Far lovelier than I.
And from his rapt description,
She loves you gloriously.

The Man prowls out each morning
To see if spring's begun.
What infinite amusement
These creatures offer one!

He asks me such conundrums
As no one ever heard:
The name of April's father,
The trail of every bird,

What keeps me warm in winter,
Who wakes me up in time,
And why procrastination
Is such a fearful crime.

And yet, who knows? He may be
Our equal ages hence—
With such pathetic glimmers
Of weird intelligence!

But this your blessed alien,
Why strays she roving here?

Was Orpheus not her brother,
Persephone her peer?

Was she not once a dryad
Whom Syrinx lulled to sleep
Beside the Dorian water,
And still her eyelids keep

The glad unperished secret
From centuries of joy,
And memories of the morning
When Helen sailed for Troy?

Is her name Gertrude, Kitty,
Hypatia, or what?
I seem to half remember,
And yet have quite forgot.

That soft Hellenic laughter!
I marvel you don't make
An effort to be early
In budding for her sake.

Just fancy hearing daily
That velvet voice of hers!
How do you quell the riot
Of sap her coming stirs?

Perhaps she puts her face up,
(Dear Charity she is!)
For messages of summer
And better worlds than this.

You cannot blush, poor Lilac;
It is not in your race.
I simply should go crimson,
If I were in your place.

Do tell her all your secrets!
The Man declares she knows
Better than any mortal
The wonder-trick of prose.

Our prose, I mean,—how beauty
Appears to you and me;
The truth that seems so simple,
Which they call poetry.

They put it down in writing
And label it with tags,
The funny conscious people
Who mask in colored rags!

They have a thing called science,
With phrases strange and pat.
My dear, can you imagine
Intelligence like that?

And when they first discover
That yellows are not greens,
They pucker up their foreheads
And ponder what it means.

And then those cave-like places,
Churches and Capitols,
Where they all come together
Like troops of talking dolls,

To govern, as they term it,
(It's really very odd!)
And have what they call worship
Of something they call God.

But Kitty, or whatever
May be her tender name,
Is more like us. She guesses
What sets the year aflame.

She knows beyond her senses;
Do tell her all you can!
The funny people need it,—
At least, so says The Man.

Good-by, dear. I must idle.
Sweet suns and happy rains!
How nice to have these humans
With their inventive brains,—

Their little scraps of paper!
They certainly evince
Remarkable discernment.
Your ever loving Quince.

AN EASTER MARKET

Today, through your Easter market
In the lazy Southern sun,
I strolled with hands in pockets
Past the flower-stalls one by one.

Indolent, dreamy, ready
For anything to amuse,
Shyfoot out for a ramble
In his oldest hat and shoes.

Roses creamy and yellow,
Azaleas crimson and white,
And the flaky fresh carnations
My Orient of delight,—

Masses and banks of blossom
That dazzle and summon the eye,
Till the buyers are half bewildered
To know what they want. Not I.

Who would not rather be artist
And slip through the crowd unseen
To gather it all in a picture
And guess what the faces mean?

So down through the chaffering darkies
I pass to the sidewalk's end,
Through the smiling gingham bonnets
With their small farm-stuff to vend.

When, hello! my dreamer, sudden
As call at the dead of night,
What sets your pulses a-quiver,
What sets your fancy alight?

Sure of it! Mayflowers, mayflowers,
Scent of the North in spring!
Out in the vernal distance,
Heart of me, whither a-wing?

"Give me some!" Clutch the first handful,
Hungering rover of earth!
How I devour and kiss them,
Beauties that brought me to birth,

Away in the great north country,
The land of the lonely sun,

Where God has few for his fellows,
And the wolves of the snowdrift run.

Once more to the frost-bound valley
Comes April with rain in her jar;
I can hear the vesper sparrow
Under the silver star.

And many and dear and gracious
Are the dreams that walk at my side
From the land of the lingering shadows,
As out of the throng I stride.

Oh, well for you, mere onlooker,
Who drift through the world's great mart!
But we of the human sorrow
Have a joy beyond your art.

DAISIES

Over the shoulders and slopes of the dune
I saw the white daisies go down to the sea,
A host in the sunshine, an army in June,
The people God sends us to set our heart free.

The bobolinks rallied them up from the dell,
The orioles whistled them out of the wood;
And all of their singing was, "Earth, it is well!"
And all of their dancing was, "Life, thou art good!"

THE MOCKING-BIRD

Hear! hear! hear!
Listen! the word
Of the mocking-bird!
Hear! hear! hear!
I will make all clear;
I will let you know
Where the footfalls go
That through the thicket and over the hill
Allure, allure.
How the bird-voice cleaves
Through the weft of leaves
With a leap and a thrill

Like the flash of a weaver's shuttle, swift and sudden and sure!

And la, he is gone—even while I turn
The wisdom of his runes to learn.
He knows the mystery of the wood,
The secret of the solitude;
But he will not tell, he will not tell,
For all he promises so well.

KARLENE

Word of a little one born in the West,—
How like a sea-bird it comes from the sea,
Out of the league-weary waters' unrest
Blown with white wings, for a token, to me!

Blown with a skriel and a flurry of plumes
(Sea-spray and flight-rapture whirled in a gleam!)
Here for a sign of the comrade that looms
Large in the mist of my love as I dream.

He with the heart of an old violin,
Vibrant at every least stir in the place,
Lyric of woods where the thrushes begin,
Wave-questing wanderer, still for a space,—

What will the child of his be (so I muse),
Wood-flower, sea-flower, star-flower rare?
Worlds here to choose from, and which will she choose,
She whose first world is an armsweep of air?

Baby Karlene, you are wondering now
Why you can't reach the great moon that you see
Just at your hand on the edge of the bough
That waves in the window-pane—how can it be?

All your world yet hardly lies out of reach
Of ten little fingers and ten little toes.
You are a seed for the sky there to teach
(And the sun and the wind and the rain) as it grows.

Just a green leaf piercing up to the day,
Pale fleck of June to come, just to be seen
Through the rough crumble of rubble and clay
Lifting its loveliness, dawn-child, Karlene!

Fragile as fairycraft, dew-dream of love,—
Never a clod that has marred the slim stalk,
Never a stone but its frail fingers move,
Bent on the blue sky and nothing can balk!

Blue sky and wind-laughters, that is thy dream.
Ah the brave days when thy leafage shall toss
High where gold noondays and sunsets a-stream
Mix with its moving and kiss it across.

There the great clouds shall go lazily by,
Coo! thee with shadows and dazzle with shine,
Drench thee with rain-guerdons, bless thee with sky,
Till all the knowledge of earth shall be thine.

Wind from the ice-floe and wind from the palm,
Wind from the mountains and wind from the lea—
How they will sing thee of tempest and calm!
How they will lure thee with tales of the sea!

What will you be in that summer, Karlene?
Apple-tree, cherry-tree, lily, or corn?
Red rose or yellow rose, gray leaf or green?
Which will you choose now the year's at its morn?

Somewhere even now in thy heart is the will,—
"I shall be Golden Rod, slender and tall—
I shall be Pond Lily, secret and still—
I shall be Sweetbriar, Queen of them all—

"I shall give shade for the weary to rest—
I shall grow flax for the naked to wear—
Figs for a feast and all comers to guest—
Wreaths that girls twine in the laugh of their hair—

"Ivy for scholars and myrtle for lovers,
Laurel for conquerors, poets, and kings—
Broad-spreading beech-boughs whose benison covers
Clamor of bird-notes and flutter of wings—

"I shall rise tall as an elm in my grace—
I shall be clothed as catalpa is clad—
Poets shall crown me with lyrics of praise—
Lovers for lure of my blossoms go mad!"

Which shall it be, baby? Guess you at all?
Only I know in the lull of the year
You have said now where your choosing shall fall,

Only you have not yet heard yourself, dear.

So, like a mocking-bird, up in the trees,
I watching wondering where you have grown,
Borrow a note from a birdfellow's glees,
Fittest to sing you, and make it my own.

Only I know as I wonder, Karlene,
Singing up here where you think me a star,
Heaven's still above me, and some one serene
Laughs in the blue sky and knows what you are.

KARLENE

Good-morning, Karlene. It's a very
Fine beautiful world we are in.
Well, you do look as ripe as a berry;
And, pardon me, such a real chin!

And may I—Ah, thank you; the pleasure
Is mine; just one kiss by your ear!—
May I introduce myself as your
Most dutiful godfather, dear?

I have fumed, like champagne that is fizzy,
To pay my respects at your door.
But the publishers keep one so busy.
Forgive my not calling before!

Karlene, you're a very small lady
To venture so far all alone;
Especially into so shady
A place as this planet has grown.

When I now, my dear, was at your age,
When nobody tried to be rich,
But lived on high thinking and porridge
(And didn't know t' other from which!),

For a girl to go out unattended
Was considered "not only unwise
And improper—" Our grandmothers ended
By lifting to heaven their eyes.

And yet even now, though it's shocking
To slander these wonderful years,

I dare say an inch of black stocking
Could set all the world by the ears.

Black, mind you, not blue! It's a trifle;
But trifling in stockings won't do;
For love has an eye like a rifle
(His bandage is slipping askew).

But there! You are simply too charming.
No doubt you'll be modern enough
(Though the speed of the world is alarming)
To win with a delicate bluff,

As we say when we're raking the chips in,
On a hand that was not over strong—
But I see you are pursing your lips in;
Perhaps I am prating too long.

Anyhow you'll be learned in isms,
And talk pterodactyls in French,
And know polyhedrons from prisms,—
Though you may not know how to retrench.

You will fall out of love with digamma
To fall in again with Delsarte;
You will make a new Syriac grammar,
And know all the popes off by heart.

What Socrates said to Xantippe
When the lash of her tongue made him grieve;
What makes the banana peel slippy;
And what the snake whispered to Eve;

The music that Nero had played him,
When Rome was touched off with a match;
Why the king let the lady upbraid him
For burning her buns in a batch;

Why Hebrew is written left-handed;
And what Venus did with her arms;
What the Conqueror said when he landed;
The acres in Horace's farms;

The use of hirundo and passer:
All this you will probe to the pith
As a freshman at Wellesley or Vassar
Or Bryn Mawr—though I prefer Smith.

You will solve every riddle in Browning;
And learn how to paddle and swim;
And save other people from drowning;
And play basket ball in the gym.

But you'll scorn to know why there's a tax on
All reading that isn't a bore,
When Mallarmé's filtered through Saxon
And the Symbolists come to the fore.

All winter you'll read mathematics
(Oh, you'll be a terrible "prod"),
And in June, at the Senior Dramatics,
You will play like a star. But it's odd,

Since you'll quote every cadence in Kipling
And Arnold (of course I mean Matt),
If you don't make a bard of some stripling
Before he knows where he is at.

I am sure you'll be lovely as Trilby,
The loveliest bud of the year;
But remember, Karlene, I shall still be
Your doting old godfather, dear.

When you hear Archimedes' conundrum,
Like enough you'll be wanting to try
Whether one little girl contra mundum
Can't lift the old thing with a pry!

You will turn up your nose at poor "Thy will,"
With a haughty agnostical sniff,
Till you find the imperative "I will"
Has a future conditional "if."

And then you will come to your senses,
And find out why women were made;
And men too; and why there are fences
All round the whole lot where you strayed,

While you wore yourself down to a shadow
Yet failed to discover your sphere;
For you'll see Adam down in the meadow
And think what a goosey you were!

And then when your classmates are singing
Once more for good-by the old glees,
And the round painted lanterns are swinging

And sputtering out in the trees,

When everything stales and withers
Except the great stars up above,
Your heartstrings will all go to smithers,
You'll just be one crumple of love.

And Adam will be such a duffer
(Dear fellow, I mean), he'll contrive,
Till you make him, to not make him suffer,
The happiest mortal alive.

Oh, it makes me too ill to continue,
Imagining how it will be
When some dapper youth comes to win you
And smiles condescension on me!

I shall loathe his immaculate breeding,
And advise you in time to refuse.
To think he will share in your reading,
And even unbutton your shoes!

And yet when for that precious laddie
Your hair is all crinkled and curled,
I guess you'll be just like your daddy,
The dearest old soul in the world!

CONCERNING KAVIN

When Kavin comes back from the barber,
Although he no longer is young,
One cheek is as soft as his heart,
And the other as smooth as his tongue.

KAVIN AGAIN.

It is not anything he says,
It's just his presence and his smile,
The blarney of his silences
That cocker and beguile.

ACROSS THE TABLE. To A. L. L.

Here's to you, Arthur! You and I
Have seen a lot of stormy weather,
Since first we clinked cups on the sly
At school together.

The winds of fate have had their will
And blown our crafts so far apart
We hardly knew if either still
Were on the chart.

But now I know the love of man
Is more than time or space or fate,
And laugh to scorn the powers that ban,
With you for mate.

It's good to have you sitting by,
Old man, to prove the world no botch,
To shame the devil with your eye
And pass the Scotch.

BARNEY McGEE

Barney McGee, there's no end of good luck in you,
Will-o'-the-wisp, with a flicker of Puck in you,
Wild as a bull-pup and all of his pluck in you,—
Let a man tread on your coat and he'll see!—
Eyes like the lakes of Killarney for clarity,
Nose that turns up without any vulgarity,
Smile like a cherub, and hair that is carroty,—
Wow, you're a rarity, Barney McGee!
Mellow as Tarragon,
Prouder than Aragon—
Hardly a paragon,
You will agree—
Here's all that's fine to you!
Books and old wine to you!
Girls be divine to you,
Barney McGee!

Lucky the day when I met you unwittingly,
Dining where vagabonds came and went flittingly.
Here's some Barbera to drink it befittingly,
That day at Silvio's, Barney McGee!
Many's the time we have quaffed our Chianti there,
Listened to Silvio quoting us Dante there,—

Once more to drink Nebiolo spumante there,
How we'd pitch Pommery into the sea!
There where the gang of us
Met ere Rome rang of us,
They had the hang of us
To a degree.
How they would trust to you!
That was but just to you.
Here's o'er their dust to you,
Barney McGee!

Barney McGee, when you're sober you scintillate,
But when you're in drink you're the pride of the intellect;
Divil a one of us ever came in till late,
Once at the bar where you happened to be—
Every eye there like a spoke in you centering,
You with your eloquence, blarney, and bantering—
All Vagabondia shouts at your entering,
King of the Tenderloin, Barney McGee!
There's no satiety
In your society
With the variety
Of your esprit.
Here's a long purse to you,
And a great thirst to you!
Fate be no worse to you,
Barney McGee!

Och, and the girls whose poor hearts you deracinate,
Whirl and bewilder and flutter and fascinate!
Faith, it's so killing you are, you assassinate,—
Murder's the word for you, Barney McGee!
Bold when they're sunny and smooth when they're showery,—
Oh, but the style of you, fluent and flowery!
Chesterfield's way, with a touch of the Bowery!
How would they silence you, Barney machree?
Naught can your gab allay,
Learned as Rabelais
(You in his abbey lay
Once on the spree).
Here's to the smile of you,
(Oh, but the guile of you!)
And a long while of you,
Barney McGee!

Facile with phrases of length and Latinity,
Like honorificabilitudinity,
Where is the maid could resist your vicinity,

Wiled by the impudent grace of your plea?
Then your vivacity and pertinacity
Carry the day with the divil's audacity;
No mere veracity robs your sagacity
Of perspicacity, Barney McGee.
When all is new to them,
What will you do to them?
Will you be true to them?
Who shall decree?
Here's a fair strife to you!
Health and long life to you!
And a great wife to you,
Barney McGee!

Barney McGee, you're the pick of gentility;
Nothing can phase you, you've such a facility;
Nobody ever yet found your utility,—
That is the charm of you, Barney McGee;
Under conditions that others would stammer in,
Still unperturbed as a cat or a Cameron,
Polished as somebody in the Decameron,
Putting the glamour on prince or Pawnee!
In your meanderin',
Love, and philanderin',
Calm as a mandarin
Sipping his tea!
Under the art of you,
Parcel and part of you,
Here's to the heart of you,
Barney McGee!

You who were ever alert to befriend a man,
You who were ever the first to defend a man,
You who had always the money to lend a man,
Down on his luck and hard up for a V!
Sure, you'll be playing a harp in beatitude
(And a quare sight you will be in that attitude)—
Some day, where gratitude seems but a platitude,
You'll find your latitude, Barney McGee.
That's no flim-flam at all,
Frivol or sham at all,
Just the plain—Damn it all,
Have one with me!
Here's luck and more to you!
Friends by the score to you,
True to the core to you,
Barney McGee!

THE SEA GYPSY

I am fevered with the sunset,
I am fretful with the bay,
For the wander-thirst is on me
And my soul is in Cathay.

There's a schooner in the offing,
With her topsails shot with fire,
And my heart has gone aboard her
For the Islands of Desire.

I must forth again to-morrow!
With the sunset I must be
Hull down on the trail of rapture
In the wonder of the sea.

SPEECH AND SILENCE

The words that pass from lip to lip
For souls still out of reach!
A friend for that companionship
That's deeper than all speech!

SECRETS

Three secrets that never were said:
The stir of the sap in the spring,
The desire of a man to a maid,
The urge of a poet to sing.

THE FIRST JULEP

I love the lazy Southern spring,
The way she melts around a chap
And lets the great magnolias fling
Their languid petals in his lap.

I love to travel down half-way
And meet her coming up the earth,

With hurdy-gurdy men who play
And make the children dance for mirth.

But best of all I love to steer
For quiet corners not too far,
Where the first juleps reappear
With fresh green mint behind the bar.

P. S. Perhaps you'll think it queer,
But I do not dislike a hint
To let the juleps disappear
And stick my nose into the mint.

A STEIN SONG

Give a rouse, then, in the Maytime
For a life that knows no fear!
Turn night-time into daytime
With the sunlight of good cheer!
For it's always fair weather
When good fellows get together,
With a stein on the table and a good song ringing clear.

When the wind comes up from Cuba
And the birds are on the wing,
And our hearts are patting juba
To the banjo of the spring,
Then it's no wonder whether
The boys will get together,
With a stein on the table and a cheer for everything.

For we're all frank-and-twenty
When the spring is in the air;
And we've faith and hope a-plenty,
And we've life and love to spare;
And it's birds of a feather
When we all get together,
With a stein on the table and a heart without a care.

For we know the world is glorious,
And the goal a golden thing,
And that God is not censorious
When his children have their fling;
And life slips its tether
When the boys get together,
With a stein on the table in the fellowship of spring.

THE UNSAINTING OF KAVIN

Saint Kavin was a gentleman,
He came from Tipperary;
And woman was the only thing
That ever made him scary.

For Kavin was a tender youth,
And he was very simple;
He feared the wiles of maiden smiles,
And fainted at a dimple.

But when Kathleen at seventeen
Came down the street one morning,
The luck of man came over him
And took him without warning.

Afraid to meet a foolish fate
By green sea or by dry land,
He fled away without delay
And sought a desert island.

But even there he felt despair;
For happiness is only
The hope of doing something else;
And he was very lonely.

He vowed to lead a life of prayer
Because that he had lost her;
And every time he thought of her
He said a Pater noster.

Yet hard it is for man to change
The less love for the greater;
And every time he reached Amen,
He must go back to Pater.

And so he grew a year or two
Disconsolate and holy,
While friends he'd known long since had grown
Papas and roly-poly.

Until one day, one blessed day,
A-moping like a Hindoo,
He saw Kathleen in mournful mien

A-passing by his window.

He threw away his rosary,
His Paters and his Aves;
For love is stronger than the wind
That wafts a thousand navies.

The holy man went forth to war,
But not against the devil.
He led the maid within for shade,
And treated her most civil.

He gave her cakes, he gave her wine,
He set his best before her;
And then invited her to dine—
Thenceforth—with her adorer.

Her little head went round for joy;
She tried to kick the rafter:
So Kavin was a saint no more,
And happy ever after.

IN THE WAYLAND WILLOWS

Once I met a soncy maid,
Soncy maid, soncy maid,
Once I met a soncy maid
In the Wayland willows.

All her hair was goldy brown,
Goldy brown, goldy brown,
In the sun a single braid
To her waist hung down.

Honey bees, honey bees,
You are roving fellows!
Idly went the doxy wind
In the Wayland willows.

There I caught her eye a-dance,
Through the catkins downy.
"Heigho, Brownie-pate," said I;
"Heigho," said my Brownie.

Then I kissed my soncy maid,
Soncy maid, soncy maid,

Kissed and kissed my soncy maid
In the Wayland willows.

Goldy eyes and goldy hair,
And little gypsy bosom,
Chin and lip and shoulder tip,
Blossom after blossom!

Hand in hand and cheek by cheek
All the morning weather!
How the yellow butterflies
Danced and winked together!

Till the day went down the hill
Where the shadows waded.
"Heigho, Soncy!" "Heigho, me!"
Then I did as day did.

All her tousled beauty bright
And teasing as before,
I left her there in sweet despair,
A soncy maid no more.

WHEN I WAS TWENTY

It was June, and I was twenty.
All my wisdom, poor but plenty,
Never learned Festina lente.
Youth is gone, but whither went he?

Madeline came down the orchard
With a mischief in her eye,
Half demure and half inviting,
Melting, wayward, wistful, shy.

Four bright eyes that found life lovely,
And forgot to wonder why;
Four warm lips at one love-lesson,
Learned by heart so easily.

We gained something of that knowledge
No man ever yet put by,
But his after days of sorrow
Left him nothing but to die.

Madeline went up the orchard,

Down the hurrying world went I;
Now I know love has no morrow,
Happiness no by-and-by.

Youth is gone, but whither went he?
All my wisdom, poor but plenty,
Never learned Festina lente.
It was June, and I was twenty.

IN A SILENCE

Heart to heart!
And the stillness of night and the moonlight, like hushed breathing
Silently, stealthily moving across thy hair!

O womanly face!
Tender and strong and lucent with infinite feeling,
Shrinking with startled joy, like wind-struck water,
And yet so frank, so unashamed of love!

Ay, for there it is, love—that's the deepest.
Love's not love in the dark.
Light loves wither i' the sun, but Love endureth,
Clothing himself with the light as with a robe.

I would bare my soul to thy sight—
Leave not a secret deep unsearched,
Unrevealing its shame or its glory.
Love without Truth shall die as a soul without God.
A lying love is the love of a day
But the brave and true shall love forever.

Build Love a house;
Let the walls be thick;
Shut him in from the sight of men;
But hide not Love from himself.

Ah, the summer night!
The wind in the trees and the moonlight!
And my kisses on thy throat
And thy breathing in my hair!

Silent, lips to lips!
But our souls have held speech, thought answering echoing thought,
Though the only words were kisses.

THE BATHER

I saw him go down to the water to bathe;
He stood naked upon the bank.

His breast was like a white cloud in the heaven, that catches the sun;
It swelled with the sharp joy of the air.

His legs rose with the spring and curve of young birches;
The hollow of his back caught the blue shadows:

With his head thrown up to the lips of the wind;
And the curls of his forehead astir with the wind.

I would that I were a man, they are so beautiful;
Their bodies are like the bows of the Indians;
They have the spring and the grace of bows of hickory.

I know that women are beautiful, and that I am beautiful;
But the beauty of a man is so lithe and alive and triumphant,
Swift as the night of a swallow and sure as the pounce of the eagle.

NOCTURNE: IN ANJOU

I dreamed of Sappho on a summer night.
Her nightingales were singing in the trees
Beside the castled river; and the wind
Fell like a woman's fingers on my cheek.
And then I slept and dreamed and marked no change;
The night went on with me into my dream.
This only I remember, that I cried:
"O Sappho! ere I leave this paradise,
Sing me one song of those lost books of yours
For which we poets still go sorrowing;
That when I meet my fellows on the earth
I may rejoice them more than many pearls;"
And she, the sweetly smiling, answered me,
As one who dreams, "I have forgotten them."

NOCTURNE: IN PROVENCE

The blue night, like an angel, came into the room,—

Came through the open window from the silent sky
Down trellised stairs of moonlight into the dear room
As if a whisper breathed of some divine one nigh.
The nightingales, like brooks of song in Paradise,
Gurgled their serene rapture to the silent sky—
Like springs of laughter bubbling up in Paradise,
The serene nightingales along the riverside
Purled low in every tree their star-cool melodies
Of joy—in every tree along the riverside.

Did the vain garments melt in music from your side?
Did you rise from them as a lily flowers i' the air?
—But you were there before me like the Night's own bride—
I dared not call you mine. So still and tall you were,
I never dreamed that you were mine—I never dreamed
I loved you—I forgot I loved you. You were air
And music, and the shadows that you stood in, seemed
Like priests that keep their sombre vigil round a shrine—
Like sombre priests that watch about a glorious shrine.

And then you stepped into the moonlight and laid bare
The wonder of your body to the night, and stood
With all the stars of heaven looking at you there,
As simply as a saint might bare her soul to God—
As simply as a saint might bathe in lakes of prayer—
Stood with the holy moonlight falling on you there
Until I thought that in a glory unaware
I had seen a soul stand forth and bare itself to God—
A saintly soul lay bare its innocence to God.

JUNE NIGHT IN WASHINGTON

The scent of honeysuckle,
Drugging the twilight
With its sweet opiate of lovers' dreams!
The last red glow of the setting sun
On the red brick wall
Of the neighboring house,
And the scramble of red roses over it!

Slowly, slowly
The night smokes up from the city to the stars,
The faint foreshadowed stars;
The smouldering night
Breathes upward like the breath
Of a woman asleep

With dim breast rising and falling
And a smile of delicate dreams.

Softly, softly
The wind comes into the garden,
Like a lover that fears lest he waken his love,
And his hands drip with the scent of the roses
And his locks weep with the opiate odor of honeysuckle.
Sighing, sighing
As a lover that yearns for the lips of his love,
In a torment of bliss,
In a passionate dreaming of bliss,
The wind in the trees of the garden!

How intimate are the trees,—
Rustling like the secret darkness of the soul!
How still is the starlight,—
Aloof in the placidity of dream!

Outside the garden
A group of negroes passing in the street
Sing with ripe lush voices,
Sing with voices that swim
Like great slow gliding fishes
Through the scent of the honeysuckle:

My love's waitin',
Waitin' by the river,
Waitin' till I come along!
Wait there, child; I'm comin'.

Jay-bird tol' me,
Tol' me in the mornin',
Tol' me she'd be there to-night.
Wait there, child; I'm comin'.

Waves of dream!
Spell of the summer night!
Will of the grass that stirs in its sleep!
Desire of the honeysuckle!
And further away,
Like the plash of far-off waves in the fluid night,
The negroes, singing:

Whip-po'-will tol' me,
Tol' me in the evenin',
"Down by the bend where the cat-tails grow."
Wait there, child; I'm comin'.

Lo, the moon,
Like a galleon sailing the night;
And the wash of the moonlight over the roofs and the trees!

Oh, my bride,
Come down from yonder lattice where you bide
Like a charmed princess in a Persian song!
I look up at your yellow window-panes,
Set in the night with far-off wizardry.
Come down, come down; the night is fain of you,
The garden waits your footstep on its walks.

Lo, the moon,
Like a galleon sailing the night;
And the wash of the moonlight over the red brick wall and the roses!

A gleam of lamplight through an open door!
A footfall like the wind's upon the grass!
A rustle like the wind's among the leaves!...
Dim as a dream of pale peach blooms of light,
Blue in the blue soft pallor of the moon,
She comes between the trees as a faint tune
Falls from a flute far off into the night....
So Death might come to one who knew him Love.

A SONG FOR MARNA

Dame of the night of hair
Like blue smoke blown!
World yet undreamed-of there
Lurks to be known.

Dame of the dizzy eyes,
Lure of dim quests!
World of what midnights lies
Under thy breasts!

Dame of the quench of love,
Give me to quaff!
There's all the world's made of
Under thy laugh.

Dame of the dare of gods,
Let the sky lower!
Time, give the world for odds,—

I choose this hour.

SEPTEMBER WOODLANDS

This is not sadness in the wood;
The yellowbird
Flits joying through the solitude,
By no thought stirred
Save of his little duskier mate
And rompings jolly.

If there's a Dryad in the wood,
She is not sad.
Too wise the spirits are to brood;
Divinely glad,
They dream with countenance sedate
Not melancholy.

NANCIBEL

The ghost of a wind came over the hill,
While day for a moment forgot to die,
And stirred the sheaves
Of the millet leaves,
As Nancibel went by.

Out of the lands of Long Ago,
Into the land of By and By,
Faded the gleam
Of a journeying dream,
As Nancibel went by.

A VAGABOND SONG.

There is something in the autumn that is native to my blood—
Touch of manner, hint of mood;
And my heart is like a rhyme,
With the yellow and the purple and the crimson keeping time.

The scarlet of the maples can shake me like a cry
Of bugles going by.
And my lonely spirit thrills

To see the frosty asters like a smoke upon the hills.

There is something in October sets the gypsy blood astir;
We must rise and follow her,
When from every hill of flame
She calls and calls each vagabond by name.

THREE OF A KIND

Three of us without a care
In the red September
Tramping down the roads of Maine,
Making merry with the rain,
With the fellow winds a-fare
Where the winds remember.

Three of us with shocking hats,
Tattered and unbarbered,
Happy with the splash of mud,
With the highways in our blood,
Bearing down on Deacon Platt's
Where last year we harbored.

We've come down from Kennebec,
Tramping since last Sunday,
Loping down the coast of Maine,
With the sea for a refrain,
And the maples neck and neck
All the way to Fundy.

Sometimes lodging in an inn,
Cosey as a dormouse—
Sometimes sleeping on a knoll
With no rooftree but the Pole—
Sometimes halely welcomed in
At an old-time farmhouse.

Loafing under ledge and tree,
Leaping over boulders,
Sitting on the pasture bars,
Hail-fellow with storm or stars—
Three of us alive and free,
With unburdened shoulders!

Three of us with hearts like pine
That the lightnings splinter,

Clean of cleave and white of grain—
Three of us afoot again,
With a rapture fresh and fine
As a spring in winter!

All the hills are red and gold;
And the horns of vision
Call across the crackling air
Till we shout back to them there,
Taken captive in the hold
Of their bluff derision.

Spray-salt gusts of ocean blow
From the rocky headlands;
Overhead the wild geese fly,
Honking in the autumn sky;
Black sinister flocks of crow
Settle on the dead lands.

Three of us in love with life,
Roaming like wild cattle,
With the stinging air a-reel
As a warrior might feel
The swift orgasm of the knife
Slay him in mid-battle.

Three of us to march abreast
Down the hills of morrow!
With a clean heart and a few
Friends to clench the spirit to!—
Leave the gods to rule the rest,
And good-by, sorrow!

WOOD-FOLK LORE. To T. B. M.

For every one
Beneath the sun,
Where Autumn walks with quiet eyes,
There is a word,
Just overheard
When hill to purple hill replies.

This afternoon,
As warm as June,
With the red apples on the bough,
I set my ear

To hark and hear
The wood-folk talking, you know how.

There comes a "Hush!"
And then a "Tush,"
As tree to scarlet tree responds,
"Babble away!
He'll not betray
The secrets of us vagabonds.

"Are we not all,
Both great and small,
Cousins and kindred in a joy
No school can teach,
No worldling reach,
Nor any wreck of chance destroy?"

And so we are,
However far
We journey ere the journey ends,
One brotherhood
With leaf and bud
And everything that wakes or wends.

The wind that blows
My autumn rose
Where Grand Pré looks to Blomidon,—
How great must be
The company
Of roses he has leaned upon,

Since first he shed
Their petals red
Through Persian gardens long ago,
When Omar heard
His muttered word
Rumoring things we may not know!

Our brother ghost,
He is a most
Incorrigible wanderer;
And still to-day
He takes his way
About my hills of spruce and fir;

Will neither bide
By the great tide,
In apple lands of Acadie,

Nor in the leaves
About your eaves,
Where Scituate looks out to sea.

AT MICHAELMAS

About the time of Michael's feast
And all his angels,
There comes a word to man and beast
By dark evangels.

Then hearing what the wild things say
To one another,
Those creatures first born of our gray
Mysterious Mother,

The greatness of the world's unrest
Steals through our pulses;
Our own life takes a meaning guessed
From the torn dulse's.

The draft and set of deep sea-tides
Swirling and flowing,
Bears every filmy flake that rides,
Grandly unknowing.

The sunlight listens; thin and fine
The crickets whistle;
And floating midges fill the shine
Like a seeding thistle.

The hawkbit flies his golden flag
From rocky pasture,
Bidding his legions never lag
Through morning's vasture.

Soon we shall see the red vines ramp
Through forest borders,
And Indian summer breaking camp
To silent orders.

The glossy chestnuts swell and burst
Their prickly houses
Agog at news which reached them first
In sap's carouses.

The long noons turn the ribstons red,
The pippins yellow;
The wild duck from his reedy bed
Summons his fellow.

The robins keep the underbrush
Songless and wary,
As though they feared some frostier hush
Might bid them tarry;

Perhaps in the great North they heard
Of silence falling
Upon the world without a word,
White and appalling.

The ash-tree and the lady-fern,
In russet frondage,
Proclaim 'tis time for our return
To vagabondage.

All summer idle have we kept;
But on a morning,
Where the blue hazy mountains slept,
A scarlet warning

Disturbs our day-dream with a start;
A leaf turns over;
And every earthling is at heart
Once more a rover.

All winter we shall toil and plod,
Eating and drinking;
But now's the little time when God
Sets folk to thinking.

"Consider," says the quiet sun,
"How far I wander;
Yet when had I not time on one
More flower to squander?"

"Consider," says the restless tide,
"My endless labor;
Yet when was I content beside
My nearest neighbor?"

So wander-lust to wander-lure,
As seed to season,
Must rise and wend, possessed and sure

In sweet unreason.

For doorstone and repose are good,
And kind is duty;
But joy is in the solitude
With shy-heart beauty.

And Truth is one whose ways are meek
Beyond foretelling;
And far his journey who would seek
Her lowly dwelling.

She leads him by a thousand heights,
Lonelily faring,
With sunrise and with eagle flights
To mate his daring.

For her he fronts a vaster fog
Than Leif of yore did,
Voyaging for continents no log
Has yet recorded.

He travels by a polar star,
Now bright, now hidden,
For a free land, though rest be far
And roads forbidden,

Till on a day with sweet coarse bread
And wine she stays him,
Then in a cool and narrow bed
To slumber lays him.

So we are hers. And, fellows mine
Of fin and feather,
By shady wood and shadowy brine,
When comes the weather

For migrants to be moving on,
By lost indenture
You flock and gather and are gone:
The old adventure!

I too have my unwritten date,
My gypsy presage;
And on the brink of fall I wait
The darkling message.

The sign, from prying eyes concealed,

Is yet how flagrant!
Here's ragged-robin in the field,
A simple vagrant.

THE MOTHER OF POETS. To H. F. H.

The typewriter ticketh no more in the twilight;
The mother of poets is sitting alone;
Only the katydid teases the noonday;
Where are the good-for-naught wanderbirds flown?

Tom's in the North with his purple impressions;
Dickon's in London a-building his fame;
Fred's in the mountains a-minding his cattle;
Kavanagh's teaching and preaching and game.

Over in Kingscroft a toiler is writing,
The boyish Old Man whom no fate ever floored;
Karl's in New York with his briefs and his logic,
That subtile mind like a velvet-sheathed sword.

Blomidon welcomes his brother in silence;
Grand Pré is luring him back to her breast;
Faint and far off are the cries of the city,
There in the country of infinite rest.

All of them turn in their wide vagabondage,
Halt and remember a place they have known,
Where the typewriter ticketh no more in the twilight,
And the mother of poets is sitting alone.

There they will surely some April forgather,
Drink once together before they depart,
One by one over the threshold of silence,
On the long trail of the wandering heart.

Fear not, little mother, there may be a region
Where poets have only to smile and keep still.
The tick of the typewriter there will be useless,
But there will be need of a motherkin still.

A GOOD BY

For love of the roving foot

And joy of the roving eye,
God send you store of morrows fair
And a good rest by and by!

IN A COPY OF BROWNING

Browning, old fellow,
Your leaves grow yellow,
Beginning to mellow
As seasons pass.
Your cover is wrinkled,
And stained and sprinkled,
And warped and crinkled
From sleep on the grass.

Is it a wine stain,
Or only a pine stain,
That makes such a fine stain
On your dull blue,—
Got as we numbered
The clouds that lumbered
Southward and slumbered
When day was through?

What is the dear mark
There like an earmark,
Only a tear mark
A woman let fall?—
As bending over
She bade me discover,
"Who plays the lover,
He loses all!"

With you for teacher
We learned love's feature
In every creature
That roves or grieves;
When winds were brawling,
Or bird-folk calling,
Or leaf-folk falling,
About our eaves.

No law must straiten
The ways they wait in,
Whose spirits greaten
And hearts aspire.

The world may dwindle,
And summer brindle,
So love but kindle
The soul to fire.

Here many a red line,
Or pencilled headline,
Shows love could wed line
To golden sense;
And something better
Than wisdom's fetter
Has made your letter
Dense to the dense.

No April robin,
Nor clacking bobbin,
Can make of Dobbin
A Pegasus;
But Nature's pleading
To man's unheeding,
Your subtile reading
Made clear to us.

You made us farers
And equal sharers
With homespun wearers
In home-made joys;
You made us princes
No plea convinces
That spirit winces
At dust and noise.

When Fate was nagging,
And days were dragging,
And fancy lagging,
You gave it scope,—
When eaves were drippy,
And pavements slippy,—
From Lippo Lippi
To Evelyn Hope.

When winter's arrow
Pierced to the marrow,
And thought was narrow,
You gave it room;
We guessed the warder
On Roland's border,
And helped to order

The Bishop's Tomb.

When winds were harshish,
And ways were marshish,
We found with Karshish
Escape at need;
Were bold with Waring
In far seafaring,
And strong in snaring
Ben Ezra's creed.

We felt the menace
Of lovers pen us,
Afloat in Venice
Devising fibs;
And little mattered
The rain that pattered,
While Blougram chattered
To Gigadibs.

And we too waited
With heart elated
And breathing bated,
For Pippa's song;
Saw Satan hover,
With wings to cover
Porphyria's lover,
Pompilia's wrong.

Long thoughts were started,
When youth departed
From the half-hearted
Riccardi's bride;
For, saith your fable,
Great Love is able
To slip the cable
And take the tide.

Or truth compels us
With Paracelsus,
Till nothing else is
Of worth at all.
Del Sarto's vision
Is our own mission,
And art's ambition
Is God's own call.

Through all the seasons,

You gave us reasons
For splendid treasons
To doubt and fear;
Bade no foot falter,
Though weaklings palter,
And friendships alter
From year to year.

Since first I sought you,
Found you and bought you,
Hugged you and brought you
Home from Cornhill,
While some upbraid you,
And some parade you,
Nine years have made you
My master still.

SHAKESPEARE HIMSELF: FOR THE UNVEILING OF MR. PARTRIDGE'S STATUE OF THE POET

The body is no prison where we lie
Shut out from our true heritage of sun;
It is the wings wherewith the soul may fly.
Save through this flesh so scorned and spat upon,
No ray of light had reached the caverned mind,
No thrill of pleasure through the life had run,
No love of nature or of humankind,
Were it but love of self, had stirred the heart
To its first deed. Such freedom as we find,
We find but through its service, not apart.
And as an eagle's wings upbear him higher
Than Andes or Himalaya, and chart
Rivers and seas beneath; so our desire,
With more celestial members yet, may soar
Into the space of empyrean fire,
Still bodied but more richly than before.

The body is the man; what lurks behind
Through it alone unveils itself. Therefore
We are not wrong, who seek to keep in mind
The form and feature of the mighty dead.
So back of all the giving is divined
The giver, back of all things done or said
The man himself in elemental speech
Of flesh and bone and sinew utterèd.

This is thy language, Sculpture. Thine to reach

Beneath all thoughts, all feelings, all desires,
To that which thinks and lives and loves, and teach
The world the primal selfhood of its sires,
Its heroes and its lovers and its gods.
So shall Apollo flame in marble fires,
The mien of Zeus suffice before he nods,
So Gautama in ivory dream out
The calm of Time's untrammelled periods,
So Sigurd's lips be in themselves a shout.

Mould us our Shakespeare, sculptor, in the form
His comrades knew, rare Ben and all the rout
That found the taproom of the Mermaid warm
With wit and wine and fellowship, the face
Wherein the men he chummed with found a charm
To make them love him; carve for us the grace
That caught Anne Hathaway in Shottery-side,
The hand that clasped Southampton's in the days
Ere that dark dame, of passion and of pride
Burned in his heart the brand of her disdain,
The eyes that wept when little Hamnet died,
The lips that learned from Marlowe's and again
Taught riper lore to Fletcher and the rest,
The presence and demeanor sovereign
At last at Stratford calm and manifest,
That rested on the seventh day and scanned
His work and knew it good, and left the quest
And like his own enchanter broke his wand.

No viewless mind! The very shape, no less,
He used to speak and smile with, move and stand!
God is most God not in his loneliness,
Unfellowed, discreationed, unrevealed,
Nor thundering on Sinai, pitiless,
Nor when the seven vials are unsealed,
But when his spirit companions with our thought
And in his fellowship our pain is healed;
And we are likest God when we are brought
Most near to all men. Bring us near to him,
The gentle, human soul whose calm might wrought
Imperious Lear and made our eyes grow dim
For Imogen,—who, though he heard the spheres
"Still choiring to the young-eyed cherubim,"
Could laugh with Falstaff and his loose compeers
And love the rascal with the same big heart
That o'er Cordelia could not stay its tears.

For still the man is greater than his art.

And though thy men and women, Shakespeare, rise
Like giants in our fancy and depart,
Thyself art more than all their masteries,
Thy wisdom more than Hamlet's questionings
Or the cold searching of Ulysses' eyes,
Thy mirth more sweet than Benedick's flouts and flings,
Thy smiling dearer than Mercutio's,
Thy dignity past that of all thy kings,
And thy enchantment more than Prospero's.

For thou couldst not have had Othello's flaw,
Not erred with Brutus,—greater, then, than those
For all their nobleness. Oh, albeit with awe,
Leave we the mighty phantoms and draw near
The man that fashioned them and gave them law!
The Master Poet found with scarce a peer
In all the ages his domain to share,
Yet of all singers gentlest and most dear!
Oh, how shall words thy proper praise declare,
Divine in thy supreme humanity
And near as the inevitable air?

So he that wrought this image deemed of thee;
So I, thy lover, keep thee in my heart;
So may this figure set for men to see
Where the world passes eager for the mart,
Be as a sudden insight of the soul
That makes a darkness into order start,
And lift thee up for all men, fair and whole,
Till scholar, merchant farmer, artisan,
Seeing, divine beneath the aureole
The fellow heart and know thee for a man.

AT THE ROAD-HOUSE: IN MEMORY OF ROBERT LOUIS STEVENSON

You hearken, fellows? Turned aside
Into the road-house of the past!
The prince of vagabonds is gone
To house among his peers at last.

The stainless gallant gentleman,
So glad of life, he gave no trace,
No hint he even once beheld
The spectre peering in his face;

But gay and modest held the road,

Nor feared the Shadow of the Dust;
And saw the whole world rich with joy,
As every valiant farer must.

I think that old and vasty inn
Will have a welcome guest to-night,
When Chaucer, breaking off some tale
That fills his hearers with delight,

Shall lift up his demure brown eyes
To bid the stranger in; and all
Will turn to greet the one on whom
The crystal lot was last to fall.

Keats of the more than mortal tongue
Will take grave Milton by the sleeve
To meet their kin, whose woven words
Had elvish music in the weave.

Dear Lamb and excellent Montaigne,
Sterne and the credible Defoe,
Borrow, DeQuincey, the great Dean,
The sturdy leisurist Thoreau;

The furtive soul whose dark romance,
By ghostly door and haunted stair,
Explored the dusty human heart
And the forgotten garrets there;

The moralist it could not spoil,
To hold an empire in his hands;
Sir Walter, and the brood who sprang
From Homer through a hundred lands,

Singers of songs on all men's lips,
Tellers of tales in all men's ears,
Movers of hearts that still must beat
To sorrows feigned and fabled tears;

Horace and Omar, doubting still
What mystery lurks beyond the seen,
Yet blithe and reassured before
That fine unvexed Virgilian mien;

These will companion him to-night,
Beyond this iron wintry gloom,
When Shakespeare and Cervantes bid
The great joy-masters give him room.

No alien there in speech or mood,
He will pass in, one traveller more;
And portly Ben will smile to see
The velvet jacket at the door.

VERLAINE

Avid of life and love, insatiate vagabond,
With quest too furious for the graal he would have won,
He flung himself at the eternal sky, as one
Wrenching his chains but impotent to burst the bond.

Yet under the revolt, the revel, the despond,
What pools of innocence, what crystal benison!
As through a riven mist that glowers in the sun,
A stretch of God's blue calm glassed in a virgin pond.

Prowler of obscene streets that riot reek along,
And aisles with incense numb and gardens mad with rose,
Monastic cells and dreams of dim brocaded lawns,

Death, which has set the calm of Time upon his song,
Surely upon his soul has kissed the same repose
In some fair heaven the Christ has set apart for Fauns.

DISTILLATION

They that eat the uncrushed grape
Walk with steady heels:
Lo, now, how they stare and gape
Where the poet reels!
He has drunk the sheer divine
Concentration of the vine.

A FRIEND'S WISH. To C. W. S.

Give me your last Aloha,
When I go out of sight,
Over the dark rim of the sea
Into the Polar night!

And all the Northland give you
Skoal for the voyage begun,
When your bright summer sail goes down
Into the zones of sun!

LAL OF KILRUDDEN

Kilrudden ford, Kilrudden dale,
Kilrudden fronting every gale
On the lorn coast of Inishfree,
And Lal's last bed the plunging sea.

Lal of Kilrudden with flame-red hair,
And the sea-blue eyes that rove and dare,
And the open heart with never a care;
With her strong brown arms and her ankles bare,
God in heaven, but she was fair,
That night the storm put in from sea?

The nightingales of Inishkill,
The rose that climbed her window-sill,
The shade that rustled or was still,
The wind that roved and had his will,
And one white sail on the low sea-hill,
Were all she knew of love.

So when the storm drove in that day,
And her lover's ship on the ledges lay,
Past help and wrecking in the gray,
And the cry was, "Who'll go down the bay,
With half of the lifeboat's crew away?"
Who should push to the front and say,
"I will be one, be others who may,"
But Lal of Kilrudden, born at sea!

The nightingales all night in the rain,
The rose that fell at her window-pane,
The frost that blackened the purple plain,
And the scorn of pitiless disdain
At the hands of the wolfish pirate main,
Quelling her great hot heart in vain,
Were all she knew of death.

Kilrudden ford, Kilrudden dale,
Kilrudden ruined in the gale

That wrecked the coast of Inishfree,
And Lal's last bed the plunging sea.

HUNTING-SONG: FROM "KING ARTHUR"

Oh, who would stay indoor, indoor,
When the horn is on the hill? (Bugle: Tarantara!
With the crisp air stinging, and the huntsmen singing,
And a ten-tined buck to kill!

Before the sun goes down, goes down,
We shall slay the buck of ten; (Bugle: Tarantara!
And the priest shall say benison, and we shall ha'e venison,
When we come home again.

Let him that loves his ease, his ease,
Keep close and house him fair; (Bugle: Tarantara!
He'll still be a stranger to the merry thrill of danger
And the joy of the open air.

But he that loves the hills, the hills,
Let him come out to-day! (Bugle: Tarantara!
For the horses are neighing, and the hounds are baying,
And the hunt's up, and away!

BUIE ANNAJOHN

Buie Annajohn was the king's black mare,
Buie, Buie, Buie Annajohn!
Satin was her coat and silk was her hair,
Buie Annajohn,
The young king's own.
March with the white moon, march with the sun,
March with the merry men, Buie Annajohn!

Buie Annajohn, when the dew lay hoar,
(Buie, Buie, Buie Annajohn!)
Down through the meadowlands went to war,—
Buie Annajohn,
The young king's own.
March by the river road, march by the dune,
March with the merry men, Buie Annajohn!

Buie Annajohn had the heart of flame,

Buie, Buie, Buie Annajohn!
First of the hosts to the hostings came
Buie Annajohn,
The young king's own.
March till we march the red sun down,
March with the merry men, Buie Annajohn!

Back from the battle at the close of day,
(Buie, Buie, Buie Annajohn!)
Came with the war cheers, came with a neigh,
Buie Annajohn,
The young king's own.
Oh, heavy was the sword that we laid on;
But half of the heave was Buie Annajohn,
Buie, Buie, Buie Annajohn!

MARY OF MARKA

Eric of Marka holds the knife:
"A nameless death for a nameless life."—

"Mary of Marka, bid him stay,
And the morrow shall be our wedding-day."—

"Will the blessing of priest give back my faith,
Or life to the child you left to death?"—

Eric of Marka holds the knife,
And turns to the mother that is no wife:

"Mary of Marka, have your will!
Shall I spare him, or shall I kill?"—

"He wrought me wrong when the days were sweet,
And he'll get no more but a winding-sheet."

PREMONITION

He said, "Good-night, my heart is light,
To-morrow morn at day
We two together in the dew
Shall forth and fare away.

"We shall go down, the halls of dawn

To find the doors of joy;
We shall not part again, dear heart."
And he laughed out like a boy.

He turned and strode down the blue road
Against the western sky
Where the last line of sunset glowed
As sullen embers die.

The night reached out her kraken arms
To clutch him as he passed,
And for one sudden moment
My soul shrank back aghast.

THE HEARSE-HORSE

Said the hearse-horse to the coffin,
"What the devil have you there?
I may trot from court to square,
Yet it neither swears nor groans,
When I jolt it over stones."
Said the coffin to the hearse-horse,
"Bones!"

Said the hearse-horse to the coffin,
"What the devil have you there,
With that purple frozen stare?
Where the devil has it been
To get that shadow grin?"
Said the coffin to the hearse-horse,
"Skin!"

Said the hearse-horse to the coffin,
"What the devil have you there?
It has fingers, it has hair;
Yet it neither kicks nor squirms
At the undertaker's terms."
Said the coffin to the hearse-horse,
"Worms!"

THE NIGHT-WASHERS

Whe-ooh, ooh, ooh, ooh, ooh!
We are the brothers of ghouls, and who

In the name of the Crooked Saints are you?

We are the washers of shrouds wherein
The lovers of beauty who sainted sin
Sleep till the Judgment Day begin.

When the moon is drifting overhead,
We wash the linen of the dead,
Stained with yellow and stiff with red.

Whe-ooh, ooh, ooh, ooh, ooh!
We are the foul night-washers, and who,
By the Seven Lovely sins are you?

Here we sit by the river reeds,
Rinsing the linen that reeks and bleeds,
And craving the help our labor needs.

Come, Sir Fop, fall to, fall to!
Show us for once what you can do!
One day there'll be washing enough for you.

Wade in, wade in, where the river runs
Clear in the moonlight over the stones!
It'll wash the ache from your scrofulous bones.

Whe-ooh, ooh, ooh, ooh, ooh!
We are the gossips of fame, and who
By the Sinners' Litany are you?

Wade in, wade in! The water is cold,
The stains are deep, and the linen is old;
But surely the sons of the town are bold!

Work for us here till the break of day
At washing the stains of the dead away,
And you shall be merry, come what may!

From now till your ninetieth year begins,
You shall sin the Seven Lovely sins,
While wearing the virtue a cardinal wins.

Refuse, and your arms shall be broken and wried,
To dangle like fenders over the side
Of an empty ship on the harbor tide!

They shall gather a waist in their grip no more,
As you wander the wide world over and o'er,

To find the doors of joy;
We shall not part again, dear heart."
And he laughed out like a boy.

He turned and strode down the blue road
Against the western sky
Where the last line of sunset glowed
As sullen embers die.

The night reached out her kraken arms
To clutch him as he passed,
And for one sudden moment
My soul shrank back aghast.

THE HEARSE-HORSE

Said the hearse-horse to the coffin,
"What the devil have you there?
I may trot from court to square,
Yet it neither swears nor groans,
When I jolt it over stones."
Said the coffin to the hearse-horse,
"Bones!"

Said the hearse-horse to the coffin,
"What the devil have you there,
With that purple frozen stare?
Where the devil has it been
To get that shadow grin?"
Said the coffin to the hearse-horse,
"Skin!"

Said the hearse-horse to the coffin,
"What the devil have you there?
It has fingers, it has hair;
Yet it neither kicks nor squirms
At the undertaker's terms."
Said the coffin to the hearse-horse,
"Worms!"

THE NIGHT-WASHERS

Who-ooh, ooh, ooh, ooh, ooh!
We are the brothers of ghouls, and who

In the name of the Crooked Saints are you?

We are the washers of shrouds wherein
The lovers of beauty who sainted sin
Sleep till the Judgment Day begin.

When the moon is drifting overhead,
We wash the linen of the dead,
Stained with yellow and stiff with red.

Whe-ooh, ooh, ooh, ooh, ooh!
We are the foul night-washers, and who,
By the Seven Lovely sins are you?

Here we sit by the river reeds,
Rinsing the linen that reeks and bleeds,
And craving the help our labor needs.

Come, Sir Fop, fall to, fall to!
Show us for once what you can do!
One day there'll be washing enough for you.

Wade in, wade in, where the river runs
Clear in the moonlight over the stones!
It'll wash the ache from your scrofulous bones.

Whe-ooh, ooh, ooh, ooh, ooh!
We are the gossips of fame, and who
By the Sinners' Litany are you?

Wade in, wade in! The water is cold,
The stains are deep, and the linen is old;
But surely the sons of the town are bold!

Work for us here till the break of day
At washing the stains of the dead away,
And you shall be merry, come what may!

From now till your ninetieth year begins,
You shall sin the Seven Lovely sins,
While wearing the virtue a cardinal wins.

Refuse, and your arms shall be broken and wried,
To dangle like fenders over the side
Of an empty ship on the harbor tide!

They shall gather a waist in their grip no more,
As you wander the wide world over and o'er,

With the curs at your heels from door to door.

With only a stranger to cover your face,
You shall die in the streets of an outcast race,
And your linen be washed in the market-place!

Whe-ooh, ooh, ooh, ooh, ooh!
We are the Scavenger Saints, but who
In the name of the Shadowy Kin are you?

MR. MOON: A SONG OF THE LITTLE PEOPLE

O Moon, Mr. Moon,
When you comin' down?
Down on the hilltop,
Down in the glen,
Out in the clearin',
To play with little men?
Moon, Mr. Moon,
When you comin' down?

O Mr. Moon,
Hurry up your stumps!
Don't you hear Bullfrog
Callin' to his wife,
And old black Cricket
A-wheezin' at his fife?
Hurry up your stumps,
And get on your pumps!
Moon, Mr. Moon,
When you comin' down?

O Mr. Moon,
Hurry up along!
The reeds in the current
Are whisperin' slow;
The river's a-wimplin'
To and fro.
Or you'll miss the song!
Moon, Mr. Moon,
When you comin' down?

O Mr. Moon,
We're all here!
Honey-bug, Thistledrift,
White-imp, Weird,

Wryface, Billiken,
Quidnunc, Queered;
We're all here,
And the coast is clear!
Moon, Mr. Moon,
When you comin' down?

O Mr. Moon,
We're the little men!
Dewlap, Pussymouse,
Ferntip, Freak,
Drink-again, Shambler,
Talkytalk, Squeak;
Three times ten
Of us little men!
Moon, Mr. Moon,
When you comin' down?

O Mr. Moon,
We're all ready!
Tallenough, Squaretoes,
Amble, Tip,
Buddybud, Heigho,
Little black Pip;
We're all ready,
And the wind walks steady!
Moon, Mr. Moon,
When you comin' down?

O Mr. Moon,
We're thirty score;
Yellowbeard, Piper,
Lieabed, Toots,
Meadowbee, Moonboy,
Bully-in-boots;
Three times more
Than thirty score.
Moon, Mr. Moon,
When you comin' down?

O Mr. Moon,
Keep your eye peeled;
Watch out to windward,
Or you'll miss the fun,
Down by the acre
Where the wheat-waves run;
Keep your eye peeled
For the open field.

Moon, Mr. Moon,
When you comin' down?

O Mr. Moon,
There's not much time!
Hurry, if you're comin',
You lazy old bones!
You can sleep to-morrow
While the Buzbuz drones;
There's not much time
Till the church bells chime.
Moon, Mr. Moon,
When you comin' down?

O Mr. Moon,
Just see the clover!
Soon we'll be going
Where the Gray Goose went
When all her money
Was spent, spent, spent!
Down through the clover,
When the revel's over!
Moon, Mr. Moon,
When you comin' down?

O Moon, Mr. Moon,
When you comin' down?
Down where the Good Folk
Dance in a ring,
Down where the Little Folk
Sing?
Moon, Mr. Moon,
When you comin' down?

HEM AND HAW

Hem and Haw were the sons of sin,
Created to shally and shirk;
Hem lay 'round and Haw looked on
While God did all the work.

Hem was a fogy, and Haw was a prig,
For both had the dull, dull mind;
And whenever they found a thing to do,
They yammered and went it blind.

Hem was the father of bigots and bores;
As the sands of the sea were they.
And Haw was the father of all the tribe
Who criticise to-day.

But God was an artist from the first,
And knew what he was about;
While over his shoulder sneered these two,
And advised him to rub it out.

They prophesied ruin ere man was made:
"Such folly must surely fail!"
And when he was done, "Do you think, my Lord,
He's better without a tail?"

And still in the honest working world,
With posture and hint and smirk,
These sons of the devil are standing by
While Man does all the work.

They balk endeavor and baffle reform,
In the sacred name of law;
And over the quavering voice of Hem
Is the droning voice of Haw.

ACCIDENT IN ART

That painter has not with a careless smutch
Accomplished his despair?—one touch revealing
All he had put of life, thought, vigor, feeling,
Into the canvas that without that touch
Showed of his love and labor just so much
Raw pigment, scarce a scrap of soul concealing!
What poet has not found his spirit kneeling
A sudden at the sound of such or such
Strange verses staring from his manuscript,
Written he knows not how, but which will sound
Like trumpets down the years? So Accident
Itself unmasks the likeness of Intent,
And ever in blind Chance's darkest crypt
The shrine-lamp of God's purposing is found.

IN A GARDEN

Thought is a garden wide and old
For airy creatures to explore,
Where grow the great fantastic flowers
With truth for honey at the core.

There like a wild marauding bee
Made desperate by hungry fears,
From gorgeous If to dark Perhaps
I blunder down the dusk of years.

AT THE END OF THE DAY

There is no escape by the river,
There is no flight left by the fen;
We are compassed about by the shiver
Of the night of their marching men.
Give a cheer!
For our hearts shall not give way.
Here's to a dark to-morrow,
And here's to a brave to-day!

The tale of their hosts is countless,
And the tale of ours a score;
But the palm is naught to the dauntless,
And the cause is more and more.
Give a cheer!
We may die, but not give way.
Here's to a silent morrow,
And here's to a stout to-day!

God has said: "Ye shall fail and perish;
But the thrill ye have felt to-night
I shall keep in my heart and cherish
When the worlds have passed in night."
Give a cheer!
For the soul shall not give way.
Here's to the greater to-morrow
That is born of a great to-day!

Now shame on the craven truckler
And the puling things that mope!
We've a rapture for our buckler
That outwears the wings of hope.
Give a cheer!
For our joy shall not give way.
Here's in the teeth of to-morrow

To the glory of to-day!

How many Canadians—how many even among the few who seek to keep themselves informed of the best in contemporary literature, who are ever on the alert for the new voices—realise, or even suspect, that this Northern land of theirs has produced a poet of whom it may be affirmed with confidence and assurance that he is of the great succession of English poets? Yet such—strange and unbelievable though it may seem—is in very truth the case, that poet being (to give him his full name) William Bliss Carman. Canada has full right to be proud of her poets, a small body though they are; but not only does Mr. Carman stand high and clear above them all—his place (and time cannot but confirm and justify the assertion) is among those men whose poetry is the shining glory of that great English literature which is our common heritage.

If any should ask why, if what has been just said is so, there has been—as must be admitted—no general recognition of the fact in the poet's home land, I would answer that there are various and plausible, if not good, reasons for it.

First of all, the poet, as thousands more of our young men of ambition and confidence have done, went early to the United States, and until recently, except for rare and brief visits to his old home down by the sea, has never returned to Canada—though for all that, I am able to state, on his own authority, he is still a Canadian citizen. Then all his books have had their original publication in the United States, and while a few of them have subsequently carried the imprints of Canadian publishers, none of these can be said ever to have made any special effort to push their sale. Another reason for the fact above mentioned is that Mr. Carman has always scorned to advertise himself, while his work has never been the subject of the log-rolling and booming which the work of many another poet has had—to his ultimate loss. A further reason is that he follows a rule of his own in preparing his books for publication. Most poets publish a volume of their work as soon as, through their industry and perseverance, they have material enough on hand to make publication desirable in their eyes. Not so with Mr. Carman, however, his rule being not to publish until he has done sufficient work of a certain general character or key to make a volume. As a result, you cannot fully know or estimate his work by one book, or two books, or even half a dozen; you must possess or be familiar with every one of the score and more volumes which contain his output of poetry before you can realise how great and how many-sided is his genius.

It is a common remark on the part of those who respond readily to the vigorous work of Kipling, or Masefield, even our own Service, that Bliss Carman's poetry has no relation to or concern with ordinary, everyday life. One would suppose that most persons who cared for poetry at all turned to it as a relief from or counter to the burdens and vexations of the daily round; but in any event, the remark referred to seems to me to indicate either the most casual acquaintance with Mr. Carman's work, or a complete misunderstanding and misapprehension of the meaning of it. I grant that you will find little or nothing in it all to remind you of the grim realities and vexing social problems of this modern existence of ours; but to say or to suggest that these things do not exist for Mr. Carman is to say or to suggest something which is the reverse of true. The truth is, he is aware of them as only one with the sensitive organism of a poet can be; but he does not feel that he has a call or mission to remedy them, and still less to sing of them. He therefore leaves the immediate problems of the day to those who choose, or are led, to occupy themselves therewith, and turns resolutely away to dwell upon those things which for him possess infinitely greater importance.

"What are they?" one who knows Mr. Carman only as, say, a lyrist of spring or as a singer of the delights of vagabondia probably will ask in some wonder. Well, the things which concern him above all, I would answer, are first, and naturally, the beauty and wonder of this world of ours, and next the mystery of the earthly pilgrimage of the human soul out of eternity and back into it again.

The poems in the present volume—which, by the way, can boast the high honor of being the very first regular Canadian edition of his work—will be evidence ample and conclusive to every reader, I am sure, of the place which

The perennial enchanted
Lovely world and all its lore

occupy in the heart and soul of Bliss Carman, as well as of the magical power with which he is able to convey the deep and unfailing satisfaction and delight which they possess for him. They, however, represent his latest period (he has had three well-defined periods), comprising selections from three of his last published volumes: The Rough Rider, Echoes from Vagabondia, and April Airs, together with a number of new poems, and do not show, except here and there and by hints and flashes, how great is his preoccupation with the problem of man's existence—

—the hidden import
Of man's eternal plight.

This is manifest most in certain of his earlier books, for in these he turns and returns to the greatest of all the problems of man almost constantly, probing, with consummate and almost unrivalled use of the art of expression, for the secret which surely, he clearly feels, lies hidden somewhere, to be discovered if one could but pierce deeply enough. Pick up Behind the Arras, and as you turn over page after page you cannot but observe how incessantly the poet's mind—like the minds of his two great masters, Browning and Whitman—works at this problem. In "Behind the Arras," the title poem; "In the Wings," "The Crimson House," "The Lodger," "Beyond the Gamut," "The Juggler"—yes, in every poem in the book—he takes up and handles the strange thing we know as, or call, life, turning it now this way, now that, in an effort to find out its meaning and purpose. He comes but little nearer success in this than do most of the rest of men, of course; but the magical and ever-fresh beauty of his expression, the haunting melody of his lines, the variety of his images and figures and the depth and range of his thought, put his searchings and ponderings in a class by themselves.

Lengthy quotation from Mr. Carman's books is not permitted here, and I must guide myself accordingly, though with reluctance, because I believe that in a study such as this the subject should be allowed to speak for himself as much as possible. In "Behind the Arras" the poet describes the passage from life to death as

A cadence dying down unto its source
In music's course,

and goes on to speak of death as

—the broken rhythm of thought and man,
The sweep and span
Of memory and hope
About the orbit where they still must grope
For wider scope,

To be through thousand springs restored, renewed,
With love imbrued,
With increments of will
Made strong, perceiving unattainment still
From each new skill.

Now follow some verses from "Behind the Gamut," to my mind the poet's greatest single achievement;

As fine sand spread on a disc of silver,
At some chord which bids the motes combine,
Heeding the hidden and reverberant impulse,
Shifts and dances into curve and line,

The round earth, too, haply, like a dust-mote,
Was set whirling her assigned sure way,
Round this little orb of her ecliptic
To some harmony she must obey.

And what of man?

Linked to all his half-accomplished fellows,
Through unfrontiered provinces to range—
Man is but the morning dream of nature,
Roused to some wild cadence weird and strange.

Here, now, are some verses from "Pulvis et Umbra," which is to be found in Mr. Carman's first book, Low Tide on Grand Pré, and in which the poet addresses a moth which a storm has blown into his window:

For man walks the world with mourning
Down to death and leaves no trace,
With the dust upon his forehead,
And the shadow on his face.

Pillared dust and fleeing shadow
As the roadside wind goes by,
And the fourscore years that vanish
In the twinkling of an eye.

"Pillared dust and fleeing shadow." Where in all our English literature will one find the life history of man summed up more briefly and, at the same time, more beautifully, than in that wonderful line? Now follows a companion verse to those just quoted, taken from "Lord of My Heart's Elation," which stands in the forefront of From the Green Book of the Bards. It may be remarked here that while the poet recurs again and again to some favorite thought or idea, it is never in the same words. His expression is always new and fresh, showing how deep and true is his inspiration. Again it is man who is pictured:

A fleet and shadowy column
Of dust and mountain rain,
To walk the earth a moment
And be dissolved again.

But while Mr. Carman's speculations upon life's meaning and the mystery of the future cannot but appeal to the thoughtful-minded, it is as an interpreter of nature that he makes his widest appeal. Bliss Carman, I must say here, and emphatically, is no mere landscape-painter; he never, or scarcely ever, paints a picture of nature for its own sake. He goes beyond the outward aspect of things and interprets or translates for us with less keen senses as only a poet whose feeling for nature is of the deepest and profoundest, who has gone to her whole-heartedly and been taken close to her warm bosom, can do. Is this not evident from these verses from "The Great Return"—originally called "The Pagan's Prayer," and for some inscrutable reason to be found only in the limited Collected Poems, issued in two stately volumes in 1905.

When I have lifted up my heart to thee,
Thou hast ever hearkened and drawn near,
And bowed thy shining face close over me,
Till I could hear thee as the hill-flowers hear.

When I have cried to thee in lonely need,
Being but a child of thine bereft and wrung,
Then all the rivers in the hills gave heed;
And the great hill-winds in thy holy tongue—

That ancient incommunicable speech—
The April stars and autumn sunsets know—
Soothed me and calmed with solace beyond reach
Of human ken, mysterious and low.

Who can read or listen to those moving lines without feeling that Mr. Carman is in very truth a poet of nature—nay, Nature's own poet? But how could he be other when, in "The Breath of the Reed" (From the Green Book of the Bards), he makes the appeal?

Make me thy priest, O Mother,
And prophet of thy mood,
With all the forest wonder
Enraptured and imbued.

As becomes such a poet, and particularly a poet whose birth-month is April, Mr. Carman sings much of the early spring. Again and again he takes up his woodland pipe, and lo! Pan himself and all his train troop joyously before us. Yet the singer's notes for all his singing never become wearied or strident; his airs are ever new and fresh; his latest songs are no less spontaneous and winning than were his first, written how many years ago, while at the same time they have gained in beauty and melody. What heart will not stir to the vibrant music of his immortal "Spring Song," which was originally published in the first Songs from Vagabondia, and the opening verses of which follow?

Make me over, mother April,
When the sap begins to stir!
When thy flowery hand delivers
All the mountain-prisoned rivers,
And thy great heart beats and quivers
To revive the days that were,
Make me over, mother April,
When the sap begins to stir!

Take my dust and all my dreaming,
Count my heart-beats one by one,
Send them where the winters perish;
Then some golden noon recherish
And restore them in the sun,
Flower and scent and dust and dreaming,
With their heart-beats every one!

That poem is sufficient in itself to prove that Bliss Carman has full right and title to be called Spring's own lyrist, though it may be remarked here that not all his spring poems are so unfeignedly joyous. Many of them indeed, have a touch, or more than a touch, of wistfulness, for the poet knows well that sorrow lurks under all joy, deep and well hidden though it may be.

Mr. Carman sings equally finely, though perhaps not so frequently, of summer and the other seasons; but as he has other claims upon our attention, I shall forbear to labor the fact, particularly as the following collection demonstrates it sufficiently. One of those other claims is as a writer of sea poetry. Few poets, it may be said, have pictured the majesty and the mystery, the beauty and the terror of the sea, better than he. His Ballads of Lost Haven is a veritable treasure-house for those whose spirits find kinship in wide expanses of moving waters. One of the best known poems in this volume is "The Gravedigger," which opens thus:

Oh, the shambling sea is a sexton old,
And well his work is done.
With an equal grave for lord and knave,
He buries them every one.

Then hoy and rip, with a rolling hip,
He makes for the nearest shore;
And God, who sent him a thousand ship,
Will send him a thousand more;
But some he'll save for a bleaching grave,
And shoulder them in to shore—
Shoulder them in, shoulder them in,
Shoulder them in to shore.

In "The City of the Sea" (Last Songs from Vagabondia) Mr. Carman speaks of the seabells sounding

The eternal cadence of sea sorrow
For Man's lot and immemorial wrong—
The lost strains that haunt the human dwelling
With the ghost of song.

Elsewhere he speaks of

The great sea, mystic and musical.

And here from another poem is a striking picture:

... the old sea
Seems to whimper and deplore
Mourning like a childless crone
With her sorrow left alone—
The eternal human cry
To the heedless passer-by.

I have said above that Mr. Carman has had three distinct periods, and intimated that the poems in the following collection are of his third period. The first period may be said to be represented by the Low Tide and Behind the Arras volumes, while the second is displayed in the three volumes of Songs from Vagabondia, which he published in association with his friend Richard Hovey. Bliss Carman was from the first too original and individual a poet to be directly influenced by anyone else; but there can be no doubt that his friendship with Hovey helped to turn him from over-preoccupation with mysteries which, for all their greatness, are not for man to solve, to an intenser realisation of the beauty and loveliness of the world about him and of the joys of human fellowship. The result is seen in such poems as "Spring Song," quoted in part above, and his perhaps equally well-known "The Joys of the Road," which appeared in the same volume with that poem, and a few verses from which follow:

Now the joys of the road are chiefly these:
A crimson touch on the hardwood trees;

A vagrant's morning wide and blue,
In early fall, when the wind walks, too;

A shadowy highway cool and brown,
Alluring up and enticing down

From rippled waters and dappled swamp,
From purple glory to scarlet pomp;

The outward eye, the quiet will,
And the striding heart from hill to hill.

Some of the finest of arman's work is contained in his elegiac or memorial poems, in which he commemorates Keats, Shelley, William Blake, Lincoln, Stevenson, and other men for whom hc has a kindred feeling, and also friends whom he has loved and lost. Listen to these moving lines from "Non Omnis Moriar," written in memory of Gleeson White, and to be found in Last Songs from Vagabondia:

There is a part of me that knows,
Beneath incertitude and fear,
I shall not perish when I pass
Beyond mortality's frontier;

But greatly having joyed and grieved,
Greatly content, shall hear the sigh
Of the strange wind across the lone
Bright lands of taciturnity.

In patience therefore I await
My friend's unchanged benign regard,—
Some April when I too shall be
Spilt water from a broken shard.

In "The White Gull," written for the centenary of the birth of Shelley in 1892, and included in By the Aurelian Wall, he thus apostrophizes that clear and shining spirit:

O captain of the rebel host,
Lead forth and far!
Thy toiling troopers of the night
Press on the unavailing fight;
The sombre field is not yet lost,
With thee for star.

Thy lips have set the hail and haste
Of clarions free
To bugle down the wintry verge
Of time forever, where the surge
Thunders and trembles on a waste
And open sea.

In "A Seamark," a threnody for Robert Louis Stevenson, which appears in the same volume, the poet hails "R.L.S." (of whose tribe he may be said to be truly one) as

The master of the roving kind,

and goes on:

O all you hearts about the world
In whom the truant gypsy blood,
Under the frost of this pale time,
Sleeps like the daring sap and flood
That dreams of April and reprieve!
You whom the haunted vision drives,

Incredulous of home and ease.
Perfection's lovers all your lives!

You whom the wander-spirit loves
To lead by some forgotten clue
Forever vanishing beyond
Horizon brinks forever new;
Our restless loved adventurer,
On secret orders come to him,
Has slipped his cable, cleared the reef,
And melted on the white sea-rim.

"Perfection's lovers all your lives." Of these, it may be said without qualification, is Bliss Carman himself.

No summary of Mr. Carman's work, however cursory, would be worthy of the name if it omitted mention of his ventures in the realm of Greek myth. From the Book of Myths is made up of work of that sort, every poem in it being full of the beauty of phrase and melody of which Mr. Carman alone has the secret. The finest poems in the book, barring the opening one, "Overlord," are "Daphne," "The Dead Faun," "Hylas," and "At Phædra's Tomb," but I can do no more here than name them, for extracts would fail to reveal their full beauty. And beauty, after all is said, is the first and last thing with Mr. Carman. As he says himself somewhere:

The joy of the hand that hews for beauty
Is the dearest solace under the sun.

And again

The eternal slaves of beauty
Are the masters of the world.

A slave—a happy, willing slave—to beauty is the poet himself, and the world can never repay him for the message of beauty which he has brought it.

Kindred to From the Book of Myths, but much more important, is Sappho: One Hundred Lyrics, one of the most successful of the numerous attempts which have been made to recapture the poems by that high priestess of song which remain to us only in fragments. Mr. Carman, as Charles G. D. Roberts points out in an introduction to the volume, has made no attempt here at translation or paraphrasing; his venture has been "the most perilous and most alluring in the whole field of poetry"—that of imaginative and, at the same time, interpretive construction. Brief quotation again would fail to convey an adequate idea of the exquisiteness of the work, and all I can do, therefore, is to urge all lovers of real poetry to possess themselves of Sappho: One Hundred Lyrics, for it is literally a storehouse of lyric beauty.

I must not fail here to speak of From the Book of Valentines, which contains some lovely things, notably "At the Great Release." This is not only one of the finest of all Mr. Carman's poems, but it is also one of the finest poems of our time. It is a love poem, and no one possessing any real feeling for poetry can read it without experiencing that strange thrill of the spirit which only the highest form of poetry can communicate. "Morning and Evening," "In an Iris Meadow," and "A letter from Lesbos" must be also mentioned. In the last named poem, Sappho is represented as writing to Gorgo, and expresses herself in these moving words:

If the high gods in that triumphant time
Have calendared no day for thee to come
Light-hearted to this doorway as of old,
Unmoved I shall behold their pomps go by—
The painted seasons in their pageantry,
The silvery progressions of the moon,
And all their infinite ardors unsubdued,
Pass with the wind replenishing the earth

Incredulous forever I must live
And, once thy lover, without joy behold,
The gradual uncounted years go by,
Sharing the bitterness of all things made.

Mention must be now made of Songs of the Sea Children, which can be described only as a collection of the sweetest and tenderest love lyrics written in our time—

—the lyric songs
The earthborn children sing,
When wild-wood laughter throngs
The shy bird-throats of spring;
When there's not a joy of the heart
But flies like a flag unfurled,
And the swelling buds bring back
The April of the world.

So perfect and complete are these lyrics that it would be almost sacrilege to quote any of them unless entire. Listen however, to these verses:

The day is lost without thee,
The night has not a star.
Thy going is an empty room
Whose door is left ajar.

Depart: it is the footfall
Of twilight on the hills.
Return: and every rood of ground
Breaks into daffodils.

There are those who will have it that Bliss Carman has been away from Canada so long that he has ceased to be, in a real sense, a Canadian. Such assume rather than know, for a very little study of his work would show them that it is shot through and through with the poet's feeling for the land of his birth. Memories of his childhood and youthful years down by the sea are still fresh in Mr. Carman's mind, and inspire him again and again in his writing. "A Remembrance," at the beginning of the present collection, may be pointed to as a striking instance of this, but proof positive is the volume, Songs from a

Northern Garden, for it could have been written only by a Canadian, born and bred, one whose heart and soul thrill to the thought of Canada. I would single out from this volume for special mention as being "Canadian" in the fullest sense "In a Grand Pré Garden," "The Keeper's Silence," "At Home and Abroad," "Killoleet," and "Above the Gaspereau," but have no space to quote from them.

But Mr. Carman is not only a Canadian, he is also a Briton; and evidence of this is his Ode on the Coronation, written on the occasion of the crowning of King Edward VII in 1902. This poem—the very existence of which is hardly known among us—ought to be put in the hands of every child and youth who speaks the English tongue, for no other, I dare maintain—nothing by Kipling, or Newbolt, or any other of our so-called "Imperial singers"—expresses more truly and more movingly the deep feeling of love and reverence which the very thought of England evokes in every son of hers, even though it may never have been his to see her white cliffs rise or to tread her storied ground:

O England, little mother by the sleepless Northern tide,
Having bred so many nations to devotion, trust, and pride,
Very tenderly we turn
With welling hearts that yearn
Still to love you and defend you,—let the sons of men discern
Wherein your right and title, might and majesty, reside.

In concluding this, I greatly fear, lamentably inadequate study, I come to the collection which follows, and which, as intimated above, represents the work of Mr. Carman's latest period. I must say at once that, while I yield to no one in admiration for Low Tide and the other books of that period, or for the work of the second period, as represented by the Songs from Vagabondia volumes, I have no hesitation in declaring that I regard the poet's work of the past few years with even higher admiration. It may not possess the force and vigor of the work which preceded it; but anything seemingly missing in that respect is more than made up for me by increased beauty and clarity of expression. The mysticism—verging, or more than verging, at times on symbolism—which marked his earlier poems, and which hung, as it were, as a veil between them and the reader, has gone, and the poet's thought or theme now lies clearly before us as in a mirror. What—to take a verse from the following pages at random—could be more pellucid, more crystal clear in expression—what indeed, could come closer to that achieving of the impossible at which every real poet must aim—than this from "In Gold Lacquer".

Gold are the great trees overhead,
And gold the leaf-strewn grass,
As though a cloth of gold were spread
To let a seraph pass.
And where the pageant should go by,
Meadow and wood and stream,
The world is all of lacquered gold,
Expectant as a dream.

The poet, happily, has fully recovered from the serious illness which laid him low some two years ago, and which for a time caused his friends and admirers the gravest concern, and so we may look forward hopefully to seeing further volumes of verse come from the press to make certain his name and fame. But if, for any reason, this should not be—which the gods forfend!—Later Poems, I dare affirm, must and will be regarded as the fine flower and crowning achievement of the genius and art of Bliss Carman.

R. H. HATHAWAY.
Toronto, 1921.

Bliss Carman – A Short Biography

William Bliss Carman was born in Fredericton, in New Brunswick on April 15th 1861. 'Bliss' was his mother's maiden name. She was descended from Daniel Bliss of Concord, Massachusetts, who was the great-grandfather to Ralph Waldo Emerson.

Carman was educated at Fredericton Collegiate School. Here, under the influence of the headmaster George Robert Parkin, he gained an appreciation of classical literature and was introduced to the poetry of many of the Pre-Raphaelites especially Dante Gabriel Rossetti and Algernon Charles Swinburne.

From here he graduated to the University of New Brunswick, obtaining his B.A. there in 1881. As is common with so many writers his first published piece was for the University magazine and for Carman that was in 1879.

England now beckoned and he spent a year at Oxford and then the University of Edinburgh (1882–1883). He returned home to Canada to work on his M.A. which he obtained from the University of New Brunswick in 1884.

Tragically his father died in January, 1885, followed by his mother in February of the following year. Carman now enrolled in Harvard University for a year. There he met and was part of a literary circle that included the American poet Richard Hovey, who would become his close friend, and later collaborator, on the successful Vagabondia poetry series. Carman and Hovey were members of the "Visionists" circle along with Herbert Copeland and F. Holland Day, who would later form the Boston publishing firm Copeland & Day and, in turn, launch Vagabondia.

After Harvard Carman briefly returned to Canada, but was back in Boston by February of 1890 saying "Boston is one of the few places where my critical education and tastes could be of any use to me in earning money. New York and London are about the only other places." However, he was unable to find work in Boston but was more successful in New York becoming the literary editor of the semi-religious New York Independent. There he helped Canadian poets get published and introduced them to a wider readership than they could receive in Canada.

However, Carman and work as an editor were not destined for a long career together and he was dismissed in 1892. There followed short stays with Current Literature, Cosmopolitan, The Chap-Book, and The Atlantic Monthly. Whilst these appointments provided the basis for a career and an income he was not suited to their demands. From 1895 he would only work as a contributor to magazines and newspapers whilst he worked on his volumes of poetry.

Carman first published a book of poetry in 1893 with Low Tide on Grand Pré. He had written the title poem in the summer of 1886 and it had (whilst he was still at Harvard) been published in the spring of 1887 by Atlantic Monthly. Despite its critical acceptance there was no Canadian company prepared to publish the volume. When an American company did so it went bankrupt. Life was becoming difficult for the young poet.

The following year was decidedly better. His partnership with Richard Hovey had given birth to Songs of Vagabondia and it was published by their friends at Copeland & Day. It was an immediate success. The young men were delighted at such a reception. It quickly sold out and was re-printed a number of times. Although these re-prints were small (usually 500-1000 copies) they were frequent.

On the back of this success they would write a further three volumes, which in their turn were almost as successful. They quickly became the center of a cult following, especially among students who empathized with the poetry's anti-materialistic themes, its celebration of personal freedom, and its glorification of comradeship."

The success of Songs of Vagabondia prompted the Boston firm, Stone & Kimball, to reissue Low Tide on Grand Pré and to hire Carman as the editor of its literary journal, The Chapbook. This ceased after a year when the company relocated and Carman expressed his desire to remain in Boston.

In 1885 Carman brought out Behind the Arras, a somewhat more serious and philosophical work centered on the premise of a long meditation using the speaker's house and its many rooms as a symbol of life and the choices to be made. However, the idea and its execution did not quite meld.

Signficantly, in 1896, Carman met Mrs Mary Perry King, who rapidly became patron, adviser and sometime lover. She put money in his pocket, and food in his mouth and, when he struck bottom, often repaired his confidence as well as helping to sell the work. She also later became his writing collaborator on two verse dramas.

Mitchell Kennerley, Carman's roommate wrote that, "On the rare occasions they had intimate relations they always advised me of by leaving a bunch of violets — Mary favorite flower — on the pillow of my bed." If her husband, Dr. King, knew of this arrangement he seems not to have objected. He was a great supporter of Carman's career and seemingly his wife's complicated involvement with that.

In 1897 Carman published Ballad of Lost Haven, a collection of poetry about the sea. Its notable poems include the macabre sea shanty, The Gravedigger. The following year, 1898, came By the Aurelian Wall, the title poem itself was an elegy to John Keats and the book a collection of formal elegies.

In 1899 his publisher, Lamson, Wolffe was taken over by the Boston firm of Small, Maynard & Co., who had also acquired the rights to Low Tide on Grand Pré. The copyrights to of his books were now held by one publisher and, in lieu of earnings, Carman took what would ultimately be a disastrous financial stake in the company.

As the century turned Carman was hard at work on what would eventually be a five-volume set of poetry; "Pans Pipes". Pan, the goat-god, was traditionally associated with poetry and the coming together of the earthly and the divine. The five volumes were all published between 1902 – 1905.

The inspiration for this came from Mary who had persuaded Carman to write in both prose and poetry about the ideas of 'unitrinianism.' This drew on the theories of François-Alexandre-Nicolas-Chéri Delsarte and was defined as a strategy of mind-body-spirit harmonization aimed at undoing the physical, psychological, and spiritual damage caused by urban modernity. The definition may be rather woolly but for Carman it resulted in some very fine work across the five-volume series. This shared belief between Mary and Carman created a further bond but did isolate him from his circle of friends.

The excellence of a number of these poems did much to install Carman as the most noted of Canadian Poets and eventually their own Poet Laureate. Among the most often quoted and printed are "The Dead Faun" (from Volume I), "Lord of My Heart's Elation" (Volume II) and many of the erotic poems from Volume III.

In the middle of publication in 1903, Small, Maynard failed and with it went all the assets Carman had tied up in the company.

Carman immediately signed with another Boston publisher, L.C. Page, who would publish seven new books of Carman poetry in this hectic period up to 1905. They released a further three books based on Carman's Transcript columns, and a prose work on Unitrinianism, The Making of Personality, that he'd written with Mary King.

Carman now felt secure enough to pursue his 'dream project,' namely a deluxe edition of his collected poetry to 1903. Page acquired the distribution rights on the condition that the book be sold privately, by subscription. Unfortunately, the demand wasn't there and it failed. Carman was deeply disappointed and lost faith in Page. However, their grip on his copyrights was absolute and sadly no further collected editions were to be published during his lifetime.

By 1904 his income was restricted and the offer to be editor-in-chief of the 10-volume project, The World's Best Poetry, was eagerly accepted.

For Carman perhaps his best years as a poet were now behind him. From 1908 he lived near the Kings' New Canaan, Connecticut, estate, that he named "Sunshine", or in the summer in a cabin in the Catskills, which he called "Moonshine."

With Literary tastes now moving away from what he could provide his income further dwindled and his health started to deteriorate.

In 1912 Carman published the final work in the Vagabondia series. Richard Hovey had died in 1900 and so this last work was purely his. It has a distinct elegiac tone as if remembering the past works themselves.

Although Carman was not politically active he did campaign during the World War One, as a member of the Vigilantes, who supported the American entry into the titanic struggle on the Allied side.

By 1920, Carman was impoverished and recovering from a near-fatal attack of tuberculosis. He returned to Canada and began to undertake a series of publicly successful and somewhat lucrative reading tours, saying "there is nothing worth talking of in book sales compared with reading. Breathless attention, crowded halls, and a strange, profound enthusiasm such as I never guessed could be,' he reported to a friend. 'And good thrifty money too. Think of it! An entirely new life for me, and I am the most surprised person in Canada.'"

On October 28th, 1921 Carman was honored at a dinner held by the newly-formed Canadian Authors' Association, at the Ritz Carlton Hotel in Montreal, where he was crowned Canada's Poet Laureate with a wreath of maple leaves.

Carman is placed among the Confederation Poets, a group that included his cousin, Charles G.D. Roberts, Archibald Lampman, and Duncan Campbell Scott. Carman was perhaps the best and is credited with the widest recognition. However, whilst the others carefully supplemented their income with writing novels and works for the magazines, or even other careers, Carman only wrote poetry together with a small amount of writing on literary ideas, philosophy, and aesthetics.

He continued his reading tours, and by 1925 had finally secured a new Canadian publisher; McClelland & Stewart (Toronto), who issued a collection of selected earlier verse and would now became his main publisher. Although they benefited from Carman's increased popularity and his revered position in Canadian literature, his former publisher L.C. Page would not relinquish its copyrights to his earlier works.

In his last years, Carman was a member of the Halifax literary and social set, The Song Fishermen and in 1927 he edited The Oxford Book of American Verse.

William Bliss Carman died of a brain hemorrhage, at the age of 68, in New Canaan on the 8th June, 1929. He was cremated in New Canaan and his ashes interred at Forest Hill Cemetery, Fredericton, with a national memorial service held at the Anglican cathedral there.

It was only a quarter of a century later, on May 13th, 1954, that a scarlet maple tree was planted at his graveside, to honour his request in the 1892 poem "The Grave-Tree":

Let me have a scarlet maple
For the grave-tree at my head,
With the quiet sun behind it,
In the years when I am dead.

Bliss Carman – A Concise Bibliography

Poetry Collections
Low Tide on Grand Pre: A Book of Lyrics (1893)
Songs from Vagabondia (1894)
A Seamark: A Threnody for Robert Louis Stevenson (1895)
Behind the Arras: A Book of the Unseen (1895)
More Songs from Vagabondia (1896)
Ballads of Lost Haven: A Book of the Sea (1897)
By the Aurelian Wall: And Other Elegies (1898)
A Winter Holiday (1899)
Last Songs from Vagabondia (1901)
Ballads and Lyrics (1902)
Ode on the Coronation of King Edward (1902)
Pipes of Pan: From the Book of Myths (1902)
Pipes of Pan: From the Green Book of the Bards (1903)
Pipes of Pan: Songs of the Sea Children (1904)
Pipes of Pan: Songs from a Northern Garden (1904)
Pipes of Pan: From the Book of Valentines (1905)

Sappho: One Hundred Lyrics (1904)
Poems (1905)
The Rough Rider: And Other Poems (1909)
A Painter's Holiday, and Other Poems (1911)
Echoes from Vagabondia (1912)
April Airs: A Book of New England Lyrics (1916)
The Man of The Marne: And Other Poems (1918)
The Vengeance of Noel Brassard: A Tale of the Acadian Expulsion (1919)
Far Horizons (1925)
Later Poems (1926)
Sanctuary: Sunshine House Sonnets (1929)
Wild Garden (1929)
Bliss Carman's Poems (1931)

Drama
Bliss Carman & Mary Perry King. Daughters of Dawn: A Lyrical Pageant of a Series of Historical Scenes for Presentation with Music and Dancing (1913)
Bliss Carman & Mary Perry King. Earth Deities: And Other Rhythmic Masques (1914)

Prose Collections
The Kinship of Nature (1904)
The Poetry of Life (1905)
The Friendship of Art (1908)
The Making of Personality (1908)
Talks on Poetry and Life; Being a Series of Five Lectures Delivered Before the University of Toronto, December 1925 (Speech). transcribed by Blanche Hume. 1926.
Bliss Carman's Scrap-Book: A Table of Contents (Pierce, Lorne, editor) (1931)

Editor
The World's Best Poetry (10 volumes) (1904)
The Oxford Book of American Verse (U.S. editor) (1927)
Carman, Bliss; Pierce, Lorne, editors (1935). Our Canadian Literature: Representative Verse, English and French.

www.ingramcontent.com/pod-product-compliance
Lightning Source LLC
Chambersburg PA
CBHW060146050426
42448CB00010B/2327